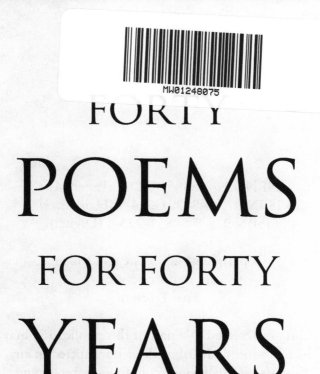

FORTY
POEMS
FOR FORTY
YEARS

GREGORY ROLLER

ISBN 979-8-88851-222-7 (Paperback)
ISBN 979-8-88851-224-1 (Hardcover)
ISBN 979-8-88851-223-4 (Digital)

Covenant Books
11661 Hwy 707
Murrells Inlet, SC 29576
www.covenantbooks.com

CONTENTS

SOMETHING MORE

Dormant has lied my passions.
With steps of fear, I tread.
My mind held as hostage
by thoughts of those now dead.

Some with lesser faculties,
or at least, do not employ,
are those with petty answers,
who live on petty joys.

But still with in me rages,
Desires that I've curtailed,
with steps of measured reason,
my longings I have jailed.

Longings for a life
that lives beyond the grave,
that laughs at lesser values,
this my soul does crave.

I want to know the secret,
The paradox of Christ,
that in dying to yourself,
you gain eternal life.

To know a joy so splendid,
the cross I will endure,
to turn my back on lesser kingdoms,
to embrace a one that's sure.

Live in the Moment

The past
an illusion
the future
contrived,
it is only in the moment
that we are alive.

So take every moment
and wring from it life.
Hold your children
more often,
make love to your
wife.

Make peace with the past,
and then let it go.
His grace is sufficient
for regrets
that you
know.

Feel the sun
on your face,
fill your chest with
the air,
pause when it's hectic,
and know he is
there.

Whatever you do,
give it all of your heart,
for it can never be done,
when this life you
depart.

Be gentle
with others,
for tomorrow
don't strive.
It is only in the moment,
that we are
alive.

By the Tracks

I met an old man
by the tracks,
whose smile,
made him turn young.
He laughed with an ease
that calmed me,
like a song that once was sung.

It seemed somehow
he knew me,
but I felt that
this couldn't be.
His years
stretched far beyond me,
as if time
had set him free.

A peace swept
suddenly through me,
like a picture,
I'd never been shown

that gives an
instant longing for a place
you know is home.

Then a train
came fast approaching,
that brought me back from where I'd been.
And I asked,
while he was smiling,
"Is this train
for you, my friend?"

For the first time,
his mouth was opened,
and he said,
"No, I'm just pass'n' through."
Then his words
mixed with the engine,
"This train,
has come for you."

The doors
were suddenly opened,
as he motioned
me inside,
and the passengers
all were smiling with nothing left to hide.

Then the train filled
with a brilliance
far brighter

than the sun,
and with a presence
that felt eternal,
like each day,
life's just begun.

The End of Time

When time doesn't matter,
and matter is no more,
when eternity, past, and future
coalesce on the same shore.

When questions become answers,
and the answers fade away,
because love will have transcended,
and all night will be as day.

When best moments are expanded,
like stars across the sky,
when the broken are made stronger,
and our loved ones never die.

When all creation sings together,
and their praises fill the skies,
and a gratitude infuses us,
because our ears will hear no cries.

When times doesn't matter,
when we will never feel alone,
when those we thought we lost,
will suddenly, welcome us back home.

OH...

Oh, this life is filled with misery,
with moments of reprieve.
So let me share some wisdom
from these words upon my sleeve.

You can take it all for granted,
and you can live with no regard,
and you can lie and say it's easy,
when you really know it's hard.

But there are moments that will mock you,
as your words fall to the floor,
when your deepest wounds are opened,
and you can't take it anymore.

Yet it's there that wisdom's waiting
to reveal its very best,
and for those with ears to listen,
your life can then be blessed.

Blessed when you have reached your end
and will finally look above
and are so completely empty
that you finally can know love.

The love that's always loved you
whether near or very far.
The kind of love that loves you
for who you really are.

The kind of love that's nearer,
much closer than a friend,
the love at your beginning
that will be there at your end.

The love that's far more stubborn
than all your greatest sins,
the kind of love that's healing,
that will always make amends.

For it's in our darkest hours
when we feel we're most alone,
that the love of God is present,
and his mercies most are shown.

ALL WILL END WELL

A child breaks the womb,
gasping for breath.
One that is old
is now sleeping in death.

And the time in between
is fleeting and brief,
filled with much striving,
sorrow, and grief.

But beauty lives on,
despite the great fall,
and a hope for much more
still lives in us all.

Just before dawn,
alone in the dark,
the mind is now waking,
its images stark.

Our past and the present,
in our memory collide
for our future,
anxiety vexes and chides.

Yet all we can do
in the midst of the gales
is plot a true course
and then set our sails.

For the wind is not ours
to have and to hold.
Its mysteries too deep,
too ancient, too old.

But the one who commands it
still rides on the storm.
His indelible image
far beyond form.

So take courage in this,
as creation will tell,
despite how things look,
all will end well.

STONES AND SAND

Her hair was thick and matted,
all tangled up and ratted,
with hard faces staring down.

Her shame was thick and sweaty,
for her punishment she was ready,
her guilt glistened on her skin.

There was no one that she trusted,
even her judges for her had lusted,
their stones now firm in hand.

But a shadow came encroaching,
it had eyes that weren't reproaching,
they stood aside to let him through.

Good teacher, we adore you,
and we humbly implore you,
should this woman live or die.

No words he had were spoken,
he refused to be their token,
he simply stooped and wrote in sand.

When he had finished writing,
the accuser's shame was biting,
they dropped their stones and walked away.

Through their judgments he had sifted,
and with gentle hands he lifted,
she was standing once again.

There is nothing I begrudge you,
and there's no one left to judge you,
please now go and sin no more.

Her heart was suddenly lighter,
something shifted deep inside her,
as he smiled and walked away.

CREATION GROANS

We know that the whole creation has been
groaning as in the pains of childbirth
right up to the present time.

—Romans 8:22

I stood by a tree
that the wind had just shaken.
All its limbs were creaking,
like it was awakened,
and it's hard to explain
what I felt in the air,
yet somehow, I knew,
the tree knew I was there.

Then I heard what sounded
like someone who's moaning.
Was it just the tree's limbs?
No, I'm sure it was groaning.

In the faintest of whispers,
It softly appealed,
"When oh when are the children revealed?"

"Children?" I said,
in a startled reply.
Was it all in my head?
Can a tree really sigh?

But the winds blew again.
Tree leaves in my face,
and it spoke once again,
"Such a desolate place."

"A desolate place?
But the fields are so green.
What are you saying?
What do you mean?"

Are these words in my head
coming from me?
Or am I actually conversing
with this ancient old tree?

Then once again,
the breeze animated
the old tree's limbs,
and it asked unabated.

"You have to know
you're his greatest creation,
and despite the great fall,
you'll be his summation."

I nervously blinked.
Could someone be there?

Have I lost my mind
now conversing with air?

Suddenly startled,
I heard the tree shout.
And I questioned no more.
There remained not a doubt.

"Me and my kind,
we've all had our fill
of subjected frustration.
That wasn't our will!!
I know you have felt it,
the mysterious groaning,
and heard of the stories
about the blood that's atoning!"

I stood there silent,
then slowly replied,
"Yes, sir, I have.
About the one that has died?"

"Is that all that you know?
all that you've heard
that it was brutal and tragic,
that death had the last word?
If I truly believed that,
then I couldn't breathe air,
I would wither and die
from relentless despair.
But death couldn't hold him,
despite giving its best.

In three days, he arose,
and creation was blessed.
From my days as a sapling
to this aged old tree,
my groanings increasing.
I so long to be free."

My eyes were now blurred
by the tears on my face.
The news was too good
my mind couldn't keep pace.

But deep in my heart,
I sensed a slight shift.
The words of this tree
had given a gift.

The first fruits of the spirit,
In my heart did abide,
and this new inward groaning,
could not be denied.

Now I'm waiting and eager,
with new hope on the rise,
for creation's release
when he appears in the skies.

Our redeemer is coming,
to protracted ovation,
for he who is worthy
of our perfect oblation.

PAYING TIME

Oh, the blustery, haughty words of youth
are tempered when we're long of tooth,
and all the advice that we ignore,
comes crashing in on times sure shore.

In youth, we spend and never think
that the waves of time will ever sink
the dreams we build with air
then suddenly, life's not fair.

That tired old man that's prone to fall,
he, too, once had a merry ball
and laughed in times gone by,
but now he's learned to cry.

Why is pride so often loud? And in our youth,
we're far too proud.
When the years will surely show,
that the strongest are brought low.

From grandest king to president
to lowly apartment resident,
to time, they're all the same,
and will extinguish every flame.

So live as brightly as you can,
but never forget you're just a man,
and that time is not impressed,
regardless of how you're dressed.

So be kind to those in aged years,
and humble when you're drinking beers,
and be grateful as you make your way,
because we all have time to pay.

AUTUMN

Summer's heat was stifling,
the sun's rage always venting.
I found myself in traffic jams
my cursing unrelenting.

Now Ms. Autumn Breeze is whispering,
and the deer have started mating.
The sun has lost its angry scowl.
His anger's now abating.

While mothers rock their little ones,
with whispers gently hushing.
The trees expose their branches,
and all the leaves are blushing.

My sweat no longer trickles down,
the cool evening now entices.
I'm reminded of my youthful days,
I smell cinnamon and spices.

Flannel tops and sweaters,
with browns of boots and saddles,
our communities are gathering,
for Friday gridiron battles.

Four seasons we are given,
and with three I'm never clear,
but with fall there are no variables,
I'm always glad you're here.

Be Humble

For all of your panting
and ranting and waste
for the dreams you have lost
and the ones you still chase.

And the hours you've spent
On knowledge in schools,
imbibing the words
of PhD fools.

Your pretentious posturing
and wringing of hands
and deft calculations
of grandiose plans

are mocked by the wisest
and the ones who will know
that even the wind
is beyond your control.

And the smallest of movements
that tick on the clock
are far more desired
than your capitalist stock.

For your money and pleasures
will come to an end,
and no one will care
about where you have been.

Or what you have done
or what you have built
or your secret confessions
of frivolous guilt.

So pause if you can,
and humble yourself,
clean out your cabinets,
and take pride from the shelf.

And maybe, just maybe,
if you really move slow,
wisdom will whisper,
and at last, you will know.

That it's not what you take
but what you will give,
and it's not what you say
but how you will live.

And that grace is a treasure
never sought by the crowd,
for it smiles on the humble
and opposes the proud.

And that God can be fierce
but still remain mild
with the face of a lion
and yet of a child.

And finally remember,
your moments will end,
so live your life fully
in the moments you're in.

MEMORIAL DAY
TRIBUTE

He was shaking but determined,
staring at beaches he'd never seen.
His face belied his age;
he was just past seventeen.

All his life he had before him,
youth fresh within his bones,
but suddenly he felt older,
when he heard the wounded's groans.

But never did he falter,
as he stepped into the waves,
his fallen brothers all around him,
who would rest in foreign graves.

It is winter in Korea;
it is cold, and he's alone,
but he thinks about his lady,
who he'll marry when he gets home.

Then suddenly, it exploded
in a brilliant flashing glow.
The dirt mixed with his blood,
turning crimson fallen snow.

He wasn't well connected.
With no politician's graft,
he couldn't hide behind deferments,
had no way to dodge the draft.

So he went when he was beckoned
while the privileged stayed behind,
and he fought deep in the jungles
as the war ravaged his mind.

With just days left in the country,
he was on his last patrol
when death demanded payment.
With his life, he paid the toll.

Raised by a single mother,
His options very few,
so he enlisted in the army
to see what he could do.

The youngest in his squad,
they were family now in arms.
While the privileged strolled at college,
they patrolled the peasants' farms.

Deep in the Korengal Valley,
the enemy hit his mark.
Fellow warriors now around him,
he lay bleeding in the dark.

He thought about his mother
and the dad he never knew,
but he was comforted while dying
by his brothers who stayed true.

In a time when things come easy
and freedom is despised,
as the talking heads keep talking,
perpetuating lies.

Step back for just a moment,
take yourself off of display,
and think about the fallen
who aren't with us here today.

Their dreams were just as precious,
and their lives no less than yours.
For freedoms you hold lightly,
they spilled their blood on distant shores.

So pause for just a moment,
stop pursuing only gain,
and be grateful for your freedoms,
so they won't have died in vain.

THE STRENGTH
OF MAN

These words that I write,
are mellowed like wine,
fermented in cellars,
from deep in my mind.

My pain and confusion,
has opened a route,
and from the ink in this pen,
my wine does spill out.

Not one word wasted,
no spurious lines,
just truth that's been tested,
by fire refined.

I have learned as a man,
you must stand alone,
and search until,
you've a strength of your own.

The woman so full,
of beauty and charm,
if pursued out of weakness,
will only do harm.

The ache in the soul,
with its desperate appeal,
to gain strength from a woman,
can never fulfill.

At first, she will comfort,
and want you around,
let you drink from her passion,
but strength won't be found.

The rush and excitement,
will soon turn to gray,
and your strength as a man,
will be given away.

What you believed was so true,
you inhaled like fresh air,
but this scent of a woman,
will turn to despair.

Her words become razors,
when she's seeking to lead
with indifference, dismiss you,
in your hour of need.

Your heart that was captured,
by her fluttering eyes,
when viewing your weakness,
will grow to despise.

All that you are,
and hoped you could be,
and pour contempt on what's left,
of your bruised dignity.

In desperation and total dismay,
you will cling and appease,
you will give her,
her way.

All of it's futile,
even if it's unfair,
but the strength of a man,
just isn't there.

And the harder you try to extract,
from her grace,
will only bring pain,
and add years to your face.

But I write not these lines,
to sever your rope,
to tear down your walls,
or vanquish your hope.

And if you will listen
to the words that I say,
it will lead to your healing,
and a much better way.

First bind up your wounds,
now steady your feet,
make vows to the Lord.
to never repeat.

The choices that's left you,
weak and despised,
yet know from these ashes,
your true strength will rise.

A man's strength is masculine,
tempered with love,
and given by grace,
from the Father above.

No woman can tell you,
that you are a man,
and your strength can't be grasped,
in a feminine hand.

Alone with the Father,
you will find the true source,
that will steady your gaze,
and mark out your course.

Then you will know,
true strength in your soul,
and you as a man,
will finally be whole.

To the woman you choose,
a true man you will be,
as you offer your strength,
from a heart that is free.

And if she is willing,
discerning, and wise,
for you alone,
will she only have eyes.

If her heart is right,
toward God and with man.
She will gladly accept,
the strength from your hand.

Then your soul will be strengthened,
but not out of lust,
but by love for a woman,
that your heart fully trust.

TRUTH

Plastic smiles and platitudes
won't take you very far
but often serve as substitutes
for how things really are.

For truth is far too precious
and can't be bent with rules,
and never will you find it
in the mouths of silly fools.

Because truth will cut you deeply,
but it will also set you free,
yet only those that recognize,
who seek it desperately.

Tragically when truth arrives,
the people often flee
or violently oppose it,
then nail it to a tree.

"What is truth?" Pilate asked
to a man standing still in place.
In his pride, he never realized
he was staring in its face.

And so the world today
is very much the same,
and those who wield the power
are often most to blame.

From CEOs to presidents,
and those in ivory towers,
who wallow in their accolades
while wasting precious hours.

Hours spent in ridicule
of those that love the way,
who never show them deference,
and from truth refuse to stray.

Those that find it better
to suffer for the right,
who reject the passing pleasures
that only last the night.

For they see him who's invisible,
who sustains and gives them breath.
The one that died to set them free
and to rescue them from death.

ETERNITY

Time, you're a liar
with the illusion of age.
You fool us to thinking
we're stuck on this stage.

This small, little stage
with you in the wing,
ticking and tocking
to minutes we cling.

But eternity beckons;
it's there in our hearts.
It knows nothing of endings
or even of starts.

It was there at our birth
When we breathed our first breath
and will be there again
when we meet our own death.

But death cannot hold us;
It's only a door
that opens up widely
and shows us there's more.

More than the minutes
that tick on the clock
or the rising and falling
of your best blue-chip stock.

For trivial matters
will then pass away,
and nighttime will cease,
and all become day.

For the creator of time,
and eternity too,
is living and moving
through all that we do.

For the years that you've lived,
and even your death,
will be swallowed up swiftly
in one massive breath.

A breath that's forever
and eternally young
is the song that's forever
that never gets sung.

For its harmony stretches
the limits of time,
transcending the moments,
going past the sublime.

Then rapturous beauty
will always exists
when the son becomes king,
and his scepter we kiss.

FATHERS AND SONS

For those who have their fathers
both far away and near,
and those who'll always miss them
and wish they were still here.

And for those who take no pleasure
when they hear their father's name.
The ones who when they hear it,
invokes an instant shame.

And to all the walking wounded,
both the fathers and the sons,
and the one who makes advances,
and the other one who shuns.

This life is often brutal,
especially for men,
who seem to live it harder,
and who bleed
from all their sin.

Just know when it is over,
and your race is finally run,
when all your rage is empty
for what's been said
and done.

It's best to show them mercy,
despite how they did live,
and to finally let it go,
and in the end,
choose to forgive.

FATE

You can scream, you can cry,
you can say how you feel.
You can grind down the hours
with a stone-grinding wheel.

But the fates are far greater,
and you just better believe
that those whom you love
may eventually leave.

The slow mundane hours,
when they feel like a bore,
and your loving them then
feels more like a chore,

may one day come haunt you
when your cupboard is bare,
and you reach out to hold them,
and they're no longer there.

So don't tempt the fates
with your insolent ways
and be grateful for love
even on the dark days.

For many would love
to have what you hold,
and would love them far better,
even when they're old.

You see, many have lost
and realized too late
that true love is rare,
and you should never tempt fate.

Providence

When I was young,
and my beard was strong,
I could wear it cropped,
or grow it long.

But now that I'm older,
with whiskers few,
I look back on,
what thought I knew.

In all my victories,
big and small,
God was the one,
behind them all.

In youthful pride,
when I felt most proud,
it was only because
that God allowed.

Whether I strolled
or decided to dance,
he controlled my times,
and circumstance.

And when I thought
it was only me
at the helm of my ship,
then he was the sea.

I controlled the rudder
and directed my knaves,
but God was the one,
who commanded the waves.

In youth, I was prideful
of common sense,
now I am humbled
by providence.

THE WARRIOR'S
RESOLVE

Forbidden fruit I've tasted,
and at times, it's made me blind,
with a lust and with a passion,
that played havoc with my mind.

In the moment it seemed so pleasing,
so easy, and so right,
any resistance I had was vanquished,
so I succumbed and lost the fight.

And wallowing in self-pity,
in regret, and deep despair,
my accuser's words were vicious,
my guilt suppressed my prayer.

But somehow in the darkness,
a whisper pierced the night,
that spoke of love and longing,
and encouraged me to fight.

The battle I lost was over,
but the war was still in sight,
and to the enemy I shouted,
I've just begun to fight.

For my Captain is far greater,
who is brighter than the sun,
who calls for me to follow,
to gain the victory he has won.

So my gaze I fix and steady,
I'll no longer believe the lies.
Despite the smoldering embers,
from these ashes I will rise.

BEWARE

Beware the man with no heaven,
who this world is all he's got,
who believes that once it's over,
his corpse is bound to rot.

There's nothing that's transcendent.
there's no eternal flame.
There are no moral absolutes,
so of course, there is no shame.

He lives for base desires,
but in pride, he claims they're more,
and just for gratification,
he makes this world his whore.

His smile is calculated.
He's plotting from the start,
in seeking satiation,
for his mercenary heart.

And weep for those poor people
when these men are on the throne,
power-hungry tyrants,
stripping freedoms to the bone.

So never believe their rhetoric
or their tunes so sweetly sung,
because deceitfulness and lies
make up their native tongue.

NIGHT RIDE

Out on a beautiful evening,
just me all alone on my bike,
I pedal with youthful exuberance.
I feel like the happiest tyke.

My hair is all ruffled and breezy.
I'm grinning with mouth open wide.
There's nothing at all to disturb me,
as I sail through the air on my ride.

Then my mouth clamps shut like a turtle.
It feels like I've swallowed a goat,
but my brain is quick to correct me.
It's only a bug down my throat.

What kind it doesn't concern me.
To me, they're just flying night things.
My coughing is loud and aggressive.
On my tongue is the taste of stale wings.

But the lesson on me is not wasted,
even though my bikes in a rut.
As so often in life and while riding,
it's better to keep your mouth shut.

UNRESTRAINED

The streams of life are moving.
No current is the same.
The words we speak are fleeting,
extinguished in life's flame.

So never take for granted
with whom you live and play,
because you have no say in when
they finally go away.

Words you wished you'd spoken,
or embraces you refrained,
will only bring you sorrow
when your tears fall unrestrained.

So remind yourself quite often,
and never believe the lie,
because even though you love them,
one day, you'll say goodbye.

Now take these words to heart, my friend,
and redeem the times that's left,
then love with pure abandon
while God still gives you breath.

LOVE WHILE
THERE'S TIME

I'm so tired of my pettiness.
Maybe time has helped my readiness
to finally tell you how I feel.

I've let my anger simmer,
my forgiveness, growing dimmer,
now I have come to let it go.

It's better late than never,
time's far past for being clever,
and you should be the first to know.

When our love was fresh and clean,
before my words were harsh and mean,
my realization dawned too slow.

But standing in the sunshine,
bright rays are cleansing my mind,
my hardened heart just melts away.

I regret the times that's wasted,
and the bitterness I've tasted,
so I stand before you here today.

It feels so liberating,
without further masquerading,
to finally tell you, you're my fave!

Yet in my sorrow I do wallow,
and my words they feel so hollow,
spoken quietly at your grave.

EAST

I watch the sky at evening light,
as fading pink,
fights with the night.

My mind has found release.

All my worries, all my pain,
just roll away,
like falling rain.

In stillness, there is peace.

No need for words, no need to talk,
I will break the hands,
on every clock.

And maybe time will cease.

I gently stroll, no need for haste,
forget the illusions,
I've often chased.

Overhead fly honking geese.

Now pink has faded from the skies
with night,
there's never compromise.

At dawn, I will face east.

CRUCIFY

You crucify him in others
when their kindness you view weak.
You crucify him in others
when you won't let weak ones speak.

You crucify him in others
when you demand you get your way.
You crucify him in others
when you kiss then you betray.

You crucify him in others
when you choose to manipulate.
You crucify him in others
when you smile to hide your hate.

You crucify him in others
when you gossip, and they're not there.
You crucify him in others
when you withhold from them their share.

You crucify him in others
when the truth you call a lie.
You crucify him in others,
and sadly, so have I.

So be done with your self-righteousness,
and on the Romans lay the blame,
because you show it in your actions,
you would have done the same.

MELTING SNOW

Snow fell early,
clean, white, and cold.
So I opened the door,
and forgot I was old.

All the white Christmases
as a kid that I missed
had returned in a moment,
on the wind, gave a kiss.

I took a deep breath,
on this magical day,
and longed for a sled
to go outside and play.

But my knees started aching,
and then a stitch in my side.
So I closed out the winter
and stepped back inside.

I mourned for my youth,
that had melted away.
Just like snow in the winter,
It, too, doesn't stay.

WISDOM

The lessons on the road of ease
are seldom ever caught,
for wisdom is despised there,
and its counsel never sought.

But for those
who've known the darkness
and have felt the sting of death,
wisdom is most valued
as precious as their breath.

Of all the schools,
that man most praise,
the ones that have the fame
can never teach the lessons
one learns inside the flame.

In the school of education,
words are written on the scroll,
but in the school of suffering,
they are written on your soul.

New Year's Eve

The night is turning colder
as the wind is turning leaves,
and I am turning inward
this frigid New Year's Eve.

The year that seemed so long
suddenly now has passed,
and the flapping ragged flag
is flying at half-mast.

I think of precious friends
both far away and near,
and the ones that I have lost
but forever still hold near.

Oh, how I do tremble
at the marching legs of time
while grasping for some hope
in my verse and in my rhyme.

At times I feel an aching
for times that now have passed
and for the loves that I have known
that I knew could never last.

But turning once again,
I face my every fear,
and with courage, reach for hope
in tomorrow's newborn year.

WIND AND FOOLS

Oh, the capricious winds of chance
that dance to time and circumstance,
calls out to masters of their fate,
who convince themselves
that they are great.
That what they are and believe to be
is nothing more than vanity.

And all they've done and so adore
was done much better,
and long before,
they learned to walk
or laugh or cry,
and before the light
had touched their eye.

Eternity had just begun
and will just begin
when their race is run.
For all their pride and verbosity

won't make a ripple on the sea,
and the waves of time will ridicule
that self-made man,
the contented fool.

A Lesson from Time

I went walking with time,
but at first didn't know
where we had started
and where we would go.

In my twenties, I was happy
and time didn't matter.
I was sure of myself
with my incessant chatter.

My thirties came creeping,
and I barely took note.
Time was irrelevant
in my prime, I did gloat.

Then my forties appeared,
and I started to pause.
I longed for a purpose,
a worthy, right cause.

Now deep in my fifties,
and time is close by.
He smiles, and he whispers,
I know you did try.

But like most of your kind,
you grasped, and you panted,
you reveled in youth,
and took me for granted.

It's only in slowing
and knowing I'm here
that the way you should travel
will ever be clear.

You see, those that live fully,
seldom do drift.
Each moment is precious,
for they know I'm a gift.

FAITH

Analogies and metaphors
can't bridge the gap between
the faith I have in what's to come
and what remains unseen.

Some will call me foolish,
and at times, I must agree,
but something still compels me.
From God's wrath, I have to flee.

I dare not flee to man's good works,
most often filled with pride
that mock the blood from the sacrifice
of the blameless one that died.

A death that's so horrific
that many do abhor.
It was not for those self-satisfied
but for sinners to their core.

To those who feel it daily,
their fallenness within
are debtors to his mercy,
and for grace that covers sin.

To those who love their glory
and repentance never show.
Who have never felt their depravity
to a savior will never go.

But to those who know they're guilty,
and from judgment's terror seek release,
take shelter in the Redeemer's ark,
and through his wounds have found their peace.

THE TRANSITION

An old man jogs
in the park today,
his stride
reveals the years,
but in his eyes a light now shines,
and his youth yet still appears.

Yes, time has
done its number,
and circumstance
has too,
but despite
their ruthless efforts,
his soul is shining through.

A soul forever
youthful,
that age
cannot contain
was purchased
by his maker
on a cross
so filled with pain.

One day soon
the tears will fall,
that would fill up
any cup,
but he whispers
as he's fading,
"I'm just now
waking up."

For those who
stand there mourning,
it's impossible to see
that the lifeless man before them
is forever youthful
and now is free.

DEEP WATERS

I just thought I was in waters deep,
but I was only off the shore,
and rolling waves were on the way
to take me down some more.

To depths I wouldn't have chosen
that I wish I could ignore,
but you're helpless when the fates arrive
and say, "We're needing more."

More than you can fathom,
and more than you would think,
the kind of more that crushes you
and takes you to the brink.

The brink where nothing matters,
where all people look the same.
To the brink where you forget your place,
and at last, forget your name.

The name you once remembered,
but now you can't recall,
the name that gets depleted
when the depths have taken all.

But I am just so tired of fighting
this futile endless war,
so I'll just release and resign myself,
and it can take me down some more.

And if I never surface,
and you see me not again,
don't weep because I'm finally home
with Jesus, who's my friend.

THE INVISIBLE

I stand upon a mountain.
The roads I've left behind.
The carnage is now clearing
from the battles in my mind.

I feel a restless spirit
like none I've known before.
I'm tired of my illusions.
I long for something more.

My allegiances have shifted
from the world and its great men,
for my heart has found one truer,
who draws closer than a friend.

His pursuit of me relentless,
his persistence unsurpassed,
and despite my frantic running,
he has captured me at last.

The scars from many clashes,
I wear upon my chest,
But in his endless mercies,
from these wounds I will be blessed.

The world and all its glory,
forever on display,
but those with eyes to see it,
it daily fades away.

Do I speak in riddles?
What do I really mean?
What we see is only temporal,
while the eternal goes unseen.

Yet all creation groans,
it longs for its release,
when the true ones are revealed,
and we will live in peace.

Pray for Me

I am just a pauper,
but syllables are free,
so I will gather and combine them,
to try and help you see.

I've been in many battles,
of many varied kind,
but none have been more vicious
than these battles in my mind.

The skies are clear above me,
yet all I feel is dread,
and though I freely walk about,
I'm a prisoner in my head.

My thoughts crush and assail me,
there is never a reprieve.
Writing brings me comfort,
but it can never quite relieve.

I've gone to the professionals
to tell them how I feel,
but their words are curt and scripted,
their answer is a pill.

I've sought the words of holy men,
who wear their religion high,
their faces hard like granite,
I'm reproved for asking why.

So my tears are spilled in darkness,
in the solitude of despair,
and if you understand this,
please say for me a prayer.

PITY

Don't pity those that suffer,
in the providence of God,
for he alone is mindful
of the path that they must trod.

You who love your luxuries
and seek to numb your pain,
who are always self-indulgent,
and pursuing only gain.

You will never feel the fire
or the refiner's many blows.
Yet you never stop to wonder,
why to you he never shows?

The glory of his majesty
or his ways within the storm,
to those quickly contented,
who prefer the average norm.

Yet to those that he's accepted
and puts through many tests,
will indeed taste this life's sorrows,
but in the end, they will be blessed.

Emerging from the flames,
their hearts are set aglow,
with his secrets he can trust them,
and his glories he will show.

So it's you that should be pitied,
who will never be so blessed,
because you settle far too quickly,
and are satisfied with less.

GRACE AND REST

How many times upon the path,
I've set my feet to go,
but waves without, and waves within,
have tossed me to and fro.

I too have boasted in my pride,
that I am not afraid,
that I will go and die with you,
and then your name betrayed.

For thirty silver pieces,
Judas failed the test,
but sadly, I have sold you out,
too often for far less.

Yet I hear you calling me,
as I hide in my despair,
with my guilt and shame condemning me,
I have no strength for prayer.

But your mercy always finds me,
as it clears away debris,
then gently you remind me,
that it's your blood that sets me free.

That all accounts were settled,
and from the cross, I have been blessed,
and works will surely follow,
when in your grace, I finally rest.

Nothing between Us

A sinner's prayer with tears,
a handshake and I'm on my way,
my Bible is open, along with my eyes,

but I just want everything to be all right between us

sins that surprise me,
the ones I didn't think I would do,
years of numbness raging,

but I just want everything to be all right between us

feel good music and laughter,
the energy of youth running free,
the days of my repentance fading,

but I just want everything to be all right between us

opinions cascading and spinning,
the doctrine police policing their doctrines,
the followers in every camp following,

but I just want everything to be all right between us

humanity reaching heights ever higher,
wars pulling down the lofty,
the clashing of ideologies exploding,

but I just want everything to be alright between us

If I know we are...okay,
I mean nothing between us but good,
like the air after a cleansing storm,

then all the rest can continue,
because I just want everything to
be all right between us.

FLINT

The raging storms have lasted
much longer than I believed,
and have blown away illusions
that my soul has deeply grieved.

I've cried to God and called to man
and cursed the night in pain,
for all that once enamored,
I now seek not to gain.

People smile with plastic grins,
heaving superficial sighs,
but my sufferings are purging,
and I detest their pretty lies.

I've stared into the eyes of loss,
and I would be remiss
if I told you that it doesn't matter,
that there is no dark abyss.

For the war is stark and deadly,
and for those it cannot tame,
it will rage in all its fury
and seek at least to maim.

Yet in this blazing battle,
strong character is made,
my resolve increases daily,
like the sharpening of a blade.

The highs and lows of pleasure
and momentary fun
have lost its sparkling luster,
like a candle in the sun.

I have my scars and my regrets,
but my will cannot be bent
because he that I hear calling,
now sets my face like flint.

KNOW THE DIFFERENCE

Knowledge is not wisdom,
no more than wet is rain,
and books can never teach you
the lessons taught through pain.

For all your facts and figures
that tip your prideful tongue
cannot produce a melody
that comforts when it's sung.

While knowledge moves so quickly,
true wisdom takes it slow,
for the pride that comes from knowing
is often gained for show.

But wisdom isn't flashy,
for its depth is far too deep.
Yes, knowledge knows the cause of death,
but can't comfort when you weep.

For all the knowledge that you seek,
so that you can come in first,
may the heat of your afflictions,
for wisdom make you thirst.

ABOUT THE AUTHOR

Gregory Roller has been many things—an airborne infantryman, a coast guardsman, a law student, and a park ranger, to name just a few, but first and fore-most, he's a sinner who hopes in God's mercy. All other titles, dispositions, and proclivities are swallowed up in the umbra of God's grace given through the gospel of his son, Jesus Christ.

Printed in the USA
CPSIA information can be obtained
at www.ICGtesting.com
LVHW091449310124
770461LV00053B/1155